Spring Evenings, Summer Afternoons

A COLLECTION OF WARM-WEATHER RECIPES

BY BARBARA SCOTT-GOODMAN

WITH MARY GOODBODY

ILLUSTRATIONS BY TOM CHRISTOPHER

CHRONICLE BOOKS

SAN FRANCISCO

For Lester,
for his love, support, and good humor

Many thanks to Bill LeBlond, Michael Carabetta, and all the wonderful people at Chronicle Books;
to my agent Bob Cornfield; to Deborah Callan for recipe testing; and especially to my collaborators,
Mary Goodbody, for her unerring good taste in food and in words; and to Tom Christopher for his
beautiful drawings. Much love and many thanks to my friends and my family, especially my daughters,
Zan and Isabelle, who have made my spring evenings and summer afternoons so happy.

Library of Congress Cataloging-in-Publication Data
Scott-Goodman, Barbara.
Spring Evenings, Summer Afternoons: a collection of warm
weather recipes / by Barbara Scott-Goodman with Mary Goodbody; illustrations by Tom Christopher.
p. cm.
Includes index.
ISBN 0-8118-0487-9
1. Cookery. 2. Spring. 3. Summer. 4. Entertaining.
TX714.s39 1994
641.5--dc20   938850
CIP

Printed in Hong Kong.

Distributed in Canada by Raincoast Books, 8680 Cambie Street, Vancouver, B.C. V6P 6M9

10 9 8 7 6 5 4 3

CHRONICLE BOOKS
275 Fifth Street
San Francisco, Ca. 94103

CONTENTS

Introduction

I love to cook, whether I am in the kitchen in our Soho loft or the kitchen in our small house in Montauk on the easternmost tip of Long Island. I am inspired not so much by specific recipes but by the food I see in the markets and the garden: The first asparagus and strawberries, fresh pink salmon, little red new potatoes, June's blueberries and July's raspberries, plump garden tomatoes, littleneck clams and glistening mussels piled high at the fish market, garden-grown basil and dill, just-picked sweet corn. These foods are so irresistible to my senses that, with my training as an artist and my instincts as a cook, I am gently and happily coaxed to prepare them. As much as tulips bobbing their heads in the spring sunshine speak of April, so does the earthy, slightly sweet flavor of asparagus. Let me take a bite of a sun-ripened peach, and I know it's high summer. This approach to cooking led me to develop the recipes in this book. I love the warm months of April and May, which gently unfold into the hotter, more sultry weeks of summer. As our children's school terms end, my husband and I wind down our life in New York and anticipate the lazy days of summer. My two young daughters and I are able to spend nearly the entire summer in Montauk. My husband contents himself with long weekends and an extended vacation. Never am I happier than when I am preparing the easy food that typifies our summery existence. The foods of spring are still vibrant in my memory—those cooked as the late-afternoon sun streamed into the windows of our Manhattan loft, promising longer days ahead. After the tantalizing freshness of spring's offerings, I am anxious to plunge into the lusciousness of summer. My favorites are reflected in these recipes. All the recipes in the book are flexible and seasonal, carefully constructed yet meant to be loose. You don't like cilantro? Use parsley or freshly snipped chives instead. Prefer more tomato in the salsa? Add a little extra. You could not find arugula in the store? Use bibb lettuce or cress in place of it. Rely on what's in the market and in your garden to inspire you.

Use what's fresh. It's up to you, as a cook, to use the very best there is to make the food as rewarding as a spring day, as spectacular as a summer sunrise.

This is a book about easy entertaining. The recipes are developed for six people—a manageable number, I think, for casual parties. If your guests are houseguests, urge them to help you wash, chop, and stir in the kitchen. Turn the trip to the fish store, farm stand, or bakery into an outing. Share the walk to the garden to pick herbs with a friend. Work together to make the meal memorable—as much for the good company during its preparation as for the time spent around the table. I love spring evenings when everyone's step is lighter, and mood giddier. These are the times I open my house and invite in friends I missed during the winter. Even more, I love summer lunches that extend into the afternoon. No time of a summer's day is more sensuous to me than the afternoon when the heat is palpable, and there's no need for any more exertion than pouring another glass of iced tea. As much as my family likes to entertain at home, we also like to pack a picnic to take to the beach late in the afternoon. Once there, we linger, eat, and talk as the sun worshippers vacate, the shadows lengthen, and the children splash in the waves. On other occasions, I fire up the grill and invite friends over for a late lunch or early supper. I appreciate the ease and informality of grilling as much as anyone, and in this book you'll find a number of recipes specifically for outdoor cooking. If you don't have a grill, use the broiler. Cooking times are the same. To me, the essence of cooking is to share good food with my family and close friends. Nothing is more rewarding and entertaining, or more satisfying, than when the delectable fruits and vegetables of spring and summer are at their best, ready to be teamed with fresh fish, chicken, or meat—and we share them with those we love.

SPRING EVENINGS

Oyster, Scallion, and Watercress Soup

Serves 6

Time was when oysters were meant only for months spelled with the letter "r."
Luckily times (and refrigeration) have changed and we can savor the briny morsels
most of the year. When stirred into this creamy soup, they add just the right touch,
making it a lovely appetizer or simple main course. It's best to buy oysters in the
shell, as I instruct, and shuck them yourself. This assures freshness and your full com-
plement of tasty oyster liquor (the liquid that escapes during shucking). If you are
pressed for time and know a reliable fish merchant, ask him to shuck them for you,
reserving the liquor. When cooking oysters, take care they do not overcook. Remove
the soup from the heat as soon as the edges of the oysters begin to curl—no later.

18 small oysters in shells, well scrubbed
2 tablespoons unsalted butter
5 to 6 scallions, trimmed and minced
4 medium carrots, peeled and cut into julienne about 1½ inches long
2 cups dry white wine
2 cups half-and-half
½ cup heavy cream
2 cups stemmed watercress (1 to 2 bunches)
Salt and freshly ground black pepper
Lemon slices, for garnish

1.   Shuck the oysters over a bowl and reserve their liquor. Strain the liquor through 1 or 2 thicknesses of dampened cheesecloth into another bowl. Set both the oysters and liquor aside.

2.   Melt the butter in a skillet over medium-high heat. Add the scallions and sauté for about 3 minutes until just softened. Set aside.

3.   Cook the carrots in boiling, salted water to cover for about 2 minutes until just tender. Drain immediately and rinse under cold water to stop the cooking. Pat them dry and set aside.

4.   In a large nonreactive saucepan or stockpot, bring the wine to a boil. Remove the pan from the heat. Slowly stir in the half-and-half and heavy cream. Stir the mixture constantly to prevent curdling. When well mixed, return the pan to the heat and bring to a slow boil. Cook uncovered over high heat for about 5 minutes until slightly thickened.

5.   Reduce the heat to medium-low and stir in the reserved oyster liquor. Add the scallions and carrots and cook for about 5 minutes until heated through. Season to taste with salt and pepper.

6.   Add the watercress and cook gently for about 5 minutes longer until heated through. Add the oysters and stir briskly for about 1 minute until their edges just begin to curl. Immediately ladle the soup into bowls and garnish by floating the lemon slices on top of the soup.

Potato, Leek, and Spinach Soup

Serves 6

The springtime green of this gently flavored soup heralds the season. It's especially welcome as an opener before a fish entrée although this soup can stand alone as a light meal with bread and a soft lettuce salad.

3 cups chicken stock, preferably homemade
1 cup water
3 russet potatoes, peeled and diced
2 tablespoons olive oil
2 tablespoons unsalted butter
1 cup thinly sliced onions (about 2 onions)
2 leeks (white and green parts), diced
About 8 ounces fresh spinach leaves, dried after washing
½ teaspoon ground nutmeg
Salt and freshly ground black pepper
1 cup milk

1.   Combine the stock, water, and potatoes in a large saucepan or stockpot. Bring to a boil and then lower the heat to medium-low. Cover and simmer for about 15 minutes until the potatoes are fork tender.

2.   Meanwhile, heat the olive oil and melt the butter in a skillet over medium heat. Add the onions and leeks and sauté for about 10 minutes stirring occasionally until tender. Add to the soup pot.

3.   Stir the spinach and nutmeg into the soup. Season to taste with salt and pepper and cook over medium heat for 1 to 2 minutes

longer until the spinach wilts and is tender. Remove the soup from the heat and let it cool for about 30 minutes.

4.   Purée the soup in a food processor or blender until smooth. If using a blender, purée the soup in batches. At this point, the soup may be refrigerated or frozen.

5.   Return the soup to the saucepan or stockpot. Stir in the milk and heat thoroughly over medium heat, stirring constantly. Adjust the seasonings and serve immediately.

Red Clam Chowder

Serves 6

Tomato-flavored clam chowder is a New York tradition. While I appreciate New England's creamier version, this red rendition is my favorite, especially in the springtime because it's so light, full-bodied, and surprisingly easy to make. When I spy tiny littleneck clams in the markets, I buy a dozen and a half and rush home to make this treat with plenty of chopped fresh parsley, onions, and garlic as well as a dash of red pepper flakes. Serve the chowder with crusty garlic bread.

¼ cup olive oil
6 cloves garlic, thinly sliced
2 cups thinly sliced onions (about 4 small onions)
1 can (28 ounces) plum tomatoes, undrained
2½ cups water
1½ cups dry white wine
¾ cup bottled clam juice
1 teaspoon dried basil
½ teaspoon dried red pepper flakes
8 small red new potatoes, cut into ½-inch dice
Salt and freshly ground black pepper
18 littleneck clams, well scrubbed
½ cup chopped fresh parsley
Parsley sprigs, for garnish

1. Heat the olive oil in a large saucepan or stockpot over medium heat. Add the garlic and onions and sauté for about 10 minutes until softened and golden. Take care the heat is low enough so that the garlic does not burn.

2.   Add the tomatoes, water, wine, clam juice, basil, and pepper flakes.
Bring to a boil, cover, reduce heat to medium low, and simmer for 20
minutes, stirring occasionally.

3.   Stir in the potatoes and bring the soup to a boil. Then reduce the
heat to medium, cover, and simmer gently for about 20 minutes until the
potatoes are tender. Season to taste with salt and pepper.

4.   When the potatoes are tender, raise the heat and bring the soup
to a boil. Add the clams and chopped parsley. Cover and cook over high
heat for 5 to 6 minutes until the clams open. Discard any unopened
clams. Ladle the soup immediately into soup bowls and garnish
with parsley sprigs.

Green Bean and Red Pepper Salad

Serves 6

If you can, use fresh green beans from your or a neighbor's garden. This is a lovely way to serve these two vegetables, particularly since the salad can be made ahead of time and served chilled or, on the other hand, made shortly before eating and served at room temperature.

1½ pounds green beans, ends trimmed
2 red bell peppers, seeded, deveined, and cut into thin strips
2 tablespoons Dijon mustard
2 tablespoons balsamic vinegar
2 teaspoons light soy sauce
½ cup olive oil
Salt and freshly ground black pepper

1. Cook the beans in enough lightly salted boiling water to cover for about 2 minutes until crisp-tender. Drain and rinse under cold running water. Drain again.

2. In another pan, cook the peppers in enough lightly salted boiling water to cover for about 3 minutes until just tender. Drain and rinse under cold running water. Drain again.

3. Combine the beans and peppers in a large ceramic or glass bowl.

4. In a small bowl, mix together the mustard, vinegar, and soy sauce. Slowly whisk in the olive oil until thick. Season the dressing to taste with salt and pepper.

5. Pour the dressing over the vegetables and toss well. Chill the salad or serve it at room temperature.

Snow Pea Salad with Walnut Vinaigrette

Serves 6

For spring gardeners, gracefully shaped snow peas are an early reward. For shoppers, fresh, local snow peas are easily available. Cook them very quickly, rinsing them under cold, running water to help them retain their bright color and crisp snap. Try to make this salad no longer than an hour or two before serving. It's best when served fresh.

1½ pounds snow peas
2 tablespoons fresh lime juice
1 tablespoon light soy sauce
½ cup walnut oil
6 scallions (white and green parts), thinly sliced on the diagonal
2 teaspoons fresh, sliced ginger root
⅓ cup coarsely chopped, lightly toasted walnuts (see Note)

1. Snap off the stem ends of the snow peas and remove the strings. Blanch the snow peas in enough boiling water to cover for about 1 minute until they turn bright green. Drain immediately and rinse with cold water to stop the cooking. Drain and set aside.

2. Whisk the lime juice and soy sauce together in a small bowl. Slowly add the walnut oil, whisking constantly, until the vinaigrette thickens.

3. Put the snow peas in a serving bowl and add the scallions, ginger, and walnuts. Toss with the vinaigrette.

Note: To toast the walnuts, spread them on a baking sheet and toast them in a preheated 350°F oven or toaster oven for about 5 minutes until golden brown. Shake the pan once or twice for even toasting. Slide the nuts off the baking sheet as soon as they reach the desired color to stop the cooking and let them cool.

Salmon Steaks in Orange-Lime Marinade

Serves 6

Delicate pink salmon steaks topped with a sprinkling of grassy-green cilantro create a tempting dish. This is quick to prepare and cooks in a matter of minutes under the broiler. I like to serve it with orzo and spring's fresh green peas.

1 teaspoon white wine vinegar
Juice of 3 oranges
Juice of 3 limes
6 cloves garlic, thinly sliced
1 teaspoon olive oil
⅓ cup finely chopped cilantro
Salt and freshly ground black pepper
6 1-inch-thick salmon steaks (about 2¼ pounds)
6 tablespoons chopped cilantro, for garnish

1.   In a shallow glass or ceramic bowl, whisk together the vinegar, orange and lime juice, and garlic. Add the olive oil, whisking until blended. Stir in the ⅓ cup cilantro and season to taste with salt and pepper. Lay the salmon steaks in the bowl and carefully turn to coat with the marinade. Cover and let the salmon marinate for 30 to 60 minutes at room temperature, turning the fish once.

2.   Preheat the broiler.

3.   Transfer the salmon and the marinade to a shallow roasting pan. Broil the salmon steaks for 5 to 6 minutes to a side until flaky but still moist.

4.   Serve each steak with a tablespoon of the cooked marinade drizzled over the top and garnish each with a tablespoon of chopped cilantro.

Lime-Marinated Cornish Game Hens

Serves 6

Tender little game hens are perfect for a spring barbecue, particularly when they are marinated in this lively lime-based marinade. Serve them on a bed of arugula accompanied with Black Bean Salad (page 42).

6 small Cornish game hens (about 1 pound each), halved
1 cup fresh lime juice (6 to 8 limes)
½ cup olive oil
4 cloves garlic, crushed
2 small onions, sliced
½ cup chopped fresh parsley
1 tablespoon herbes de Provence or 1 teaspoon
each dried tarragon, thyme, and marjoram
Salt and freshly ground black pepper
2 bunches arugula, stems removed

1. Lay the game hens in a large, shallow glass or ceramic bowl. Mix together the lime juice, olive oil, garlic, onions, parsley, and herbs and season with salt and pepper to taste. Pour the marinade over the game hens and turn them several times to coat thoroughly. Cover the bowl and refrigerate for 4 to 6 hours, turning the hens several times.

2. Preheat the oven to 350°F.

3. Transfer the marinated hens and about half the marinade to a shallow baking pan. Reserve the rest of the marinade for basting. Bake them for 35 minutes. Meanwhile prepare a charcoal or gas grill or preheat the broiler, if separate from your oven.

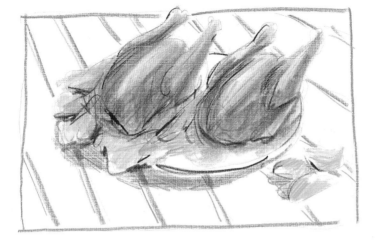

4.   Lift the hens from the marinade and grill or broil for about 10 minutes to a side about 6 to 8 inches from the heat until nicely browned and the juices run clear when the hens are pricked with a fork. Baste them often with the marinade during grilling. Serve the grilled hens on a bed of arugula.

Pork Loin with
Orange Marmalade Glaze

Serves 6

For a succulent, flavorful roast, few meats surpass pork loin. It's low in fat, cooks in less than two hours, and, best of all, melds with any number of basting sauces and glazes. I particularly like this sweet orange glaze. I serve the pork loin with spring vegetables and tiny new potatoes. It is a lovely alternative to ham or lamb for Easter dinner.

I boneless center-cut pork loin (3¼ to 4 pounds)
I tablespoon olive oil
Salt and freshly ground black pepper
2 teaspoons fresh rosemary leaves or I teaspoon dried rosemary
I cup dry white wine
I cup water
½ cup orange marmalade

1. Preheat the oven to 350°F.

2. Put the pork loin on a rack in a shallow roasting pan. Brush meat with the olive oil and then sprinkle it with salt, pepper, and rosemary. Pour the wine and water into the roasting pan. Roast for 1 hour.

3. Remove the pan from the oven and spoon ½ cup of pan drippings into a small bowl. Add the marmalade and mix well. Pour this mixture over the meat and return it to the oven.

4. Continue roasting the meat for 35 to 45 minutes, basting it 2 to 3 times with pan drippings, until a meat thermometer reaches 160°F.

5. Let the meat rest for 15 minutes before serving. Skim any fat from the pan drippings and serve with the roast.

Linguine with Smoked Salmon and Asparagus

Serves 6

Both salmon and asparagus are elegant harbingers of spring and how better to enjoy them than in this pasta dish, which, to me, is the very essence of the season? As an artist, I particularly appreciate the vibrant green of the asparagus mingled with the soft pink of the salmon against a canvas of creamy pasta.

1 pound fresh asparagus, trimmed and cut into 2-inch lengths
2 tablespoons olive oil
2 cloves garlic, thinly sliced
⅓ cup chopped shallots
1 cup heavy cream
1½ pounds fresh or dried linguine
¾ cup freshly grated Parmesan cheese
Salt and freshly ground black pepper
1 teaspoon fresh lemon juice
6 thin slices smoked salmon (3 to 4 ounces total), sliced into small pieces
Freshly grated Parmesan cheese, for garnish

1. Drop the asparagus into a saucepan of rapidly boiling water and cook for 2 minutes until al dente and bright green. Drain and set aside.

2. Heat the olive oil in a skillet over medium-low heat. Sauté the garlic and shallots for about 5 minutes until softened; take care the garlic does not burn. Add the cream and cook over low heat for about 5 minutes until thickened. Remove the skillet from the heat and set aside.

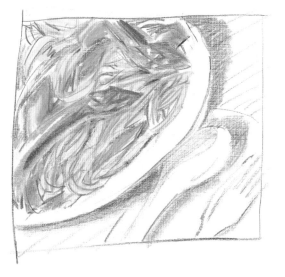

3.   Bring a large saucepan of lightly salted water to a rolling boil and cook the linguine until tender. If the linguine is fresh, this will take 2 to 3 minutes; if dried, allow 8 to 10 minutes or follow the package instructions. Drain but do not rinse the pasta. Return the hot linguine to the saucepan.

4.   Heat the cream sauce over medium heat until it begins to bubble around the edges. Pour it over the hot pasta and toss to coat well. Gently toss in the cooked asparagus, the ¾ cup grated Parmesan, salt and pepper to taste, lemon juice, and sliced salmon. Serve immediately with more freshly grated Parmesan cheese.

Asparagus Vinaigrette

Serves 6

With forsythia and daffodils, asparagus is one of the first sure signs of spring. If asparagus are thick, it is worth the effort to peel the white or woody sections. Simply snap the tough part off and peel the stalks about halfway up with a vegetable peeler. If the asparagus are slender, there is no need to peel them. Thick or slender, the key to good flavor is freshness, not size. I think one of the best ways to serve asparagus is chilled with a simple vinaigrette. Pure elegance.

2½ pounds asparagus, trimmed and peeled, if necessary
1 to 2 cloves garlic, finely minced
¼ teaspoon salt
1 tablespoon Dijon mustard
1 tablespoon red wine vinegar
⅓ cup fresh lemon juice (2 to 3 lemons)
1 cup olive oil
Freshly ground black pepper
½ cup finely chopped fresh parsley, for garnish

1. Lay the asparagus spears in a skillet large enough to hold them in a single layer. If necessary, use 2 skillets. Add enough boiling water to cover. Bring the water back to a boil, reduce the heat, and simmer for about 4 minutes until asparagus is just tender. Run cold water over the asparagus and then drain on paper towels. When drained, arrange the asparagus in a shallow serving dish.

2. In a small bowl, mix together the garlic, salt, mustard, and vinegar to make a paste. Whisk in the lemon juice and oil until blended. Season to taste with pepper. Pour the dressing over the asparagus.

3. Chill the dressed asparagus thoroughly. Garnish with parsley before serving.

Grilled Yams

Serves 6

Ever since I discovered grilled vegetables, I have been devising ways to prepare them. The first time I tried these yams, I knew I had hit on something special. Try them with barbecued chicken or grilled fish. Even though yams may not be an expected warm weather food, I promise they will be a major success.

2 pounds yams (about 4 medium yams)
¼ cup corn oil
3 tablespoons light soy sauce
¼ cup rice wine vinegar
¾ cup extra-virgin olive oil
4 scallions (white and green parts), minced
2 tablespoons chopped fresh parsley
I tablespoon finely chopped fresh ginger root
Chopped fresh parsley, for garnish

1. Bring a large pot of lightly salted water to a boil and cook the yams for about 15 minutes until just tender. Drain and rinse under cold, running water.

2. When the yams are cool enough to handle, peel and cut into ¼-inch slices. Lay the slices in a single layer in a shallow pan or on a tray.

3. In a small bowl, whisk the corn oil with 2 tablespoons of the soy sauce. Brush this over the yams.

4. In the same bowl, whisk the vinegar with the olive oil and remaining tablespoon of soy sauce. Stir in the scallions, parsley, and ginger. Set the vinaigrette aside.

5. Prepare a charcoal or gas grill. When the coals are medium hot, brush the grill rack with corn oil to keep the yams from sticking. Grill the yams for about 10 minutes, turning them often, until just tender.

6. Lift the yams from the grill and put them in a shallow serving bowl or on a platter. Drizzle the reserved vinaigrette over the yams. Garnish with fresh parsley and serve immediately.

Buttery Pastry Dough

Makes one 9-inch pie shell and top or one 12-inch tart shell

This pie pastry is easy to make in the food processor but I have given the old-fashioned hand method as an alternative. If you plan only to use it for a 9-inch bottom crust, reserve about a third of the dough for another pastry, to make a lattice top for another pie, or to make small, individual tartlets.

1¾ cups unbleached all-purpose flour
1 teaspoon salt
10 tablespoons (1¼ sticks) unsalted butter, chilled
1 tablespoon vegetable shortening, chilled
5 to 8 tablespoons ice water

1. Put the flour and salt in the bowl of a food processor. Cut the chilled butter and shortening into pieces and add them to the food processor.

2. Pulse the food processor 4 to 5 times to break up the fat. With the food processor running, add 5 tablespoons of the ice water. Turn the food processor off and then pulse it 5 or 6 times. The dough should begin to mass on the blade. If not, add another tablespoon of water, or more as needed. When the dough holds together in a cohesive mass, it is done; do not overmix.

3. Turn the dough out onto the countertop. Flatten it with the palm of your hand, dust it lightly with flour, and wrap the dough in plastic wrap or waxed paper. Chill for 1 to 2 hours before rolling out according to directions in the pie or tart recipes.

Old-Fashioned Method

1. In a large bowl, whisk together the flour and salt. Using a knife, a pastry blender, or your fingertips, blend the chilled butter and shortening into the dry ingredients until the mixture resembles coarse crumbs.

2. Sprinkle 2 tablespoons of the ice water over the flour and toss to distribute evenly. Add more water, a tablespoon at a time, tossing until the dough holds together when pressed between your fingertips. Gather it into a cohesive mass.

3. Turn the dough out onto the countertop. Flatten it with the palm of your hand into a disk shape, dust it lightly with flour, and wrap the dough in plastic wrap or waxed paper. Chill for 1 to 2 hours before rolling out according to directions in the pie or tart recipes.

Blueberry Tart

Serves 6 to 8

As much as blooming roses and fading lilac bushes, the arrival of fresh, plump blueberries in the markets is a sure sign that spring is deepening into summer. While there are numerous ways to enjoy the first berries of the season—baked into muffins, sprinkled over cereal, frozen in ice cream—a simple blueberry tart is one of the very best. For a little extra indulgence, serve the tart with whipped cream or crème fraîche.

Buttery Pastry Dough, preceding
3½ cups fresh blueberries
¼ teaspoon ground cinnamon
¼ cup sugar
3 tablespoons unsalted butter, melted
1 tablespoon fresh lemon juice
Whipped cream or crème fraîche, optional

1. Roll the pastry dough into a 14-inch circle on a sheet of waxed paper or a countertop lightly dusted with flour. Carefully lift the dough and press it into a 12-inch tart pan with a removable bottom. Trim the edges of the dough and crimp them with a fork or your fingertips. Cover the tart shell with plastic wrap and freeze for 30 minutes.

2. Preheat the oven to 425°F.

3. In a large bowl, toss the blueberries with the cinnamon, sugar, melted butter, and lemon juice. Spoon the berries into the chilled tart shell, distributing them evenly. If it's easier, slide the tart pan onto a rimless baking sheet to transport it to the oven.

4.   Bake for 10 minutes. Reduce the heat to 350°F and bake for 10 to 15 minutes longer until the berries are slightly soft. Let the tart cool before serving with whipped cream or crème fraîche, if desired.

Strawberry Rhubarb Sundaes

Serves 6

When I get the chance, I love to take my daughters strawberry picking at local farms on Long Island. As much as we enjoy the outing, we inevitably arrive home with more berries than we can eat at one time. No problem. The season is so short, I relish the opportunity to use strawberries in as many ways as I can. I came up with this simple sauce for sundaes, which the girls think are lots of fun. It's also good over other flavors of ice cream or yogurt, over pound cake or fruit sorbet, or as a topping for fresh berries. It freezes well, too, for as long as a month.

2 cups finely diced fresh rhubarb (2 to 3 large stalks)
1 pint strawberries, hulled and halved
⅓ cup water
⅓ cup crème de cassis or black currant jelly
⅓ cup sugar
6 scoops vanilla ice cream or frozen vanilla yogurt
6 large strawberries with stems, for garnish

1. Put the rhubarb, strawberries, water, crème de cassis, and sugar in a large, nonreactive saucepan. Bring to a boil over high heat, stirring. Lower the heat and simmer, uncovered, for 20 to 30 minutes until the mixture thickens, stirring occasionally. The sauce will be textured.

2. Let the sauce cool to tepid or cool room temperature, or refrigerate it for later use. The sauce may be refrigerated for 2 to 3 days or frozen for up to 1 month at this point.

3.   Put a scoop of ice cream or yogurt in a pretty dessert bowl. Spoon the sauce over the ice cream and top with a large strawberry.
Repeat to make 6 sundaes.

SUMMER AFTERNOONS

Carrot Soup with Fresh Chives

Serves 6

This is a delicate, creamy soup flavored with fresh chives and a nibble of cayenne. It makes a lovely lunch or elegant starter for a summer supper.

2 tablespoons unsalted butter
3 medium-size white onions, chopped
3 cups chicken stock, preferably homemade
1 cup water
6 large carrots, peeled and diced
5 to 6 medium-size new potatoes, peeled and diced
Pinch cayenne pepper
½ cup minced chives
Salt and freshly ground black pepper
½ cup heavy cream

1. Melt the butter in a stockpot set over medium heat. Add the onion and sauté for about 5 minutes until softened.

2. Add the stock, water, carrots, and potatoes. Bring to a boil, reduce the heat, and simmer partially covered for about 20 minutes until the vegetables are tender. Remove the pot from the heat and let the soup cool for about 1 hour.

3. Purée the soup in batches in a blender or a food processor fitted with the steel blade.

4. When all the soup is puréed, return it to the pot. Season with the cayenne, chives, and salt and pepper to taste.

5. Stir in the cream and reheat gently over low heat. Serve immediately.

Shrimp, Corn, and Potato Soup

Serves 6

*When you spend the summer on the tip of Long Island, as I do, anything made
with seafood tastes right. Trips to the fish markets are inspiring, which is how I
came to develop this lovely soup. Spotting fresh shrimp, still in their shells
(they're apt to be fresher that way), I sensed this soup would taste right. But
as long as the shrimp are fresh, the soup will taste just as right in the middle
of the plains or high on a mountaintop, served as a starter or as a main
course. My favorite garnish for it is cilantro, but if you prefer, sprinkle the soup
with garden-fresh chives or chopped parsley.*

1 tablespoon olive oil
1 tablespoon unsalted butter
2 leeks (white and green parts), diced
4 cups chicken stock, preferably homemade
2 cups water
2 pounds red new potatoes (about 8 potatoes), quartered
1 pound medium shrimp in shells, peeled and deveined, shells reserved
1 cup half-and-half
2 cups fresh corn kernels (from about 2 ears sweet corn)
Freshly ground black pepper
Finely chopped cilantro, for garnish

1. Heat the olive oil and butter in a skillet. When the butter melts, add
the leeks and cook over low heat for about 10 minutes until softened.

2. Transfer the leeks to a stockpot. Add the stock, water, and potatoes.
Stir gently.

3.   Wrap the reserved shrimp shells in cheesecloth tied with kitchen twine. Bring the soup to a boil and drop the cheesecloth pouch in the pot. Reduce the heat to medium, cover, and simmer the soup for 15 to 20 minutes until the potatoes are tender.

4.   Remove the cheesecloth pouch and discard. Add the half-and-half and cook over medium heat for about 5 minutes until heated through. Add the shrimp, corn, and pepper to taste. Cook for about 5 minutes until the shrimp turn pink.

5.   Ladle the soup into shallow soup bowls and garnish with chopped cilantro. Serve immediately.

Black Bean Salad

Serves 6

While three-bean salad has been an American summertime favorite for years, black bean salad may be a new idea to some folks. When the deep, rich-looking black beans are tossed with colorful red peppers, red onions, and scallions, they assume a refreshing summery appeal. Make this ahead of time (be sure to allow time for soaking the beans) and enjoy it with grilled chicken or fish. I love the flavor of cilantro (also called fresh coriander or Chinese parsley), but if you prefer, toss the salad with fresh flat-leaf parsley instead. If you make this more than a few hours ahead of time, you may want to refresh the beans with a little more vinaigrette or a drizzle of olive oil. As they sit, beans absorb liquid and can get a little dry.

3 cups dried black beans
6 cups chicken stock, preferably homemade
1 tablespoon Dijon mustard
2 tablespoons balsamic vinegar
2 cloves garlic, finely minced
¾ cup extra-virgin olive oil
Salt and freshly ground black pepper
1 red bell pepper, seeded, deveined, and cut into ¼-inch dice
4 scallions (white and green parts), trimmed and cut into ½-inch pieces
1 medium-size red onion, thinly sliced
½ cup chopped cilantro

1. Pick over beans, discarding any broken or misshapen ones and rinse thoroughly. Put the beans in a large pot or bowl, cover by about 2 inches with cold water, and soak for 6 to 8 hours or overnight. Change the water once or twice during soaking, if possible.

2. Drain the beans and put them in a large soup pot. Add the chicken stock and bring to a boil over high heat. Reduce the heat, cover, and simmer the beans for 45 to 60 minutes until just tender. Be careful not to overcook.

3. Drain the beans and rinse them under cold, running water. Set aside in a large bowl to cool.

4. In a small bowl, combine the mustard, vinegar, and garlic. Slowly whisk in the olive oil until thick. Season the vinaigrette to taste with salt and pepper.

5. Add the red pepper, scallions, red onion, and cilantro to the cooled beans. Toss gently. Pour the vinaigrette over the beans and toss well. Set aside for at least 1 hour to give the flavors time to blend. Or cover and refrigerate the salad for up to 12 hours before serving chilled or at room temperature.

Lobster Salad with Tomatoes and Basil

Serves 6

For a very special summer lunch, try this lobster salad—a palette of pink, red, and green. I suggest tearing the basil leaves rather than chopping them; they taste better and are less likely to bruise. After you make the salad and it's chilling, head for the bakery for a crusty baguette to serve with it.

2 live lobsters (1½ pounds each) or 2 cups cooked,
cooled, and cubed lobster meat
1 tablespoon mayonnaise
1 tablespoon Dijon mustard
1 tablespoon balsamic vinegar
Salt and freshly ground black pepper
1 cup olive oil
Juice of ½ lemon
1 teaspoon dried herbes de Provence or ½ teaspoon *each*
dried tarragon and thyme
1 cup coarsely chopped tomatoes (about 2 large tomatoes)
½ cup torn fresh basil
1 bunch arugula, stems removed
Fresh basil leaves, for garnish

1. To cook live lobsters, plunge them head first into a large pot of vigorously boiling, salted water. Cover the pot and cook over high heat for 10 minutes. Remove the pot from the heat and let stand for 15 minutes. Drain the lobsters and let them cool.

2. When cool enough to handle, crack the lobster shells and remove the meat from the claws and tail. Chop meat (it will yield about 2 cups) and chill. Reserve the rest of the lobster to make soup or discard.

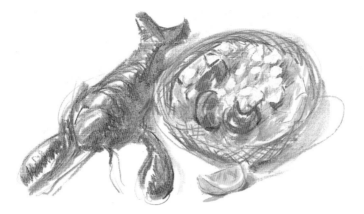

3. In a bowl large enough to hold the salad, mix together the mayonnaise, mustard, vinegar, and salt and pepper to taste. Slowly whisk in the olive oil, beating vigorously. Beat in the lemon juice and dried herbs.

4. Add the lobster, tomatoes, and basil to the bowl and toss gently to coat with dressing. Chill for 1 hour.

5. Serve the salad on beds of arugula and garnish with fresh basil leaves.

Roasted Red Potato Salad with Arugula and Goat Cheese

Serves 6

There are a few tricks to making this absolutely smashing roasted potato salad, the most important of which is to roast the potatoes very slowly. The slow cooking gives the garlic and olive oil time to infuse the potatoes with their enticing flavors. It's equally important to use the best coarse, grainy mustard you can find for the vinaigrette and to mix it with the potatoes while they are still nice and warm. Finally, while it's acceptable (practical, actually) to use ordinary olive oil to cook the potatoes, fruity, green extra-virgin olive oil is best for the dressing and for the final drizzle over the crumbled white goat cheese and peppery arugula. And of course if you don't particularly like arugula, substitute another spring green such as cress or bibb lettuce.

Potatoes:

3 pounds small red new potatoes (about 12 potatoes),
halved or quartered, depending on size
8 unpeeled cloves garlic
Coarse salt
⅓ cup olive oil

Vinaigrette:

2 teaspoons grainy mustard
1 tablespoon balsamic vinegar
½ cup extra-virgin olive oil

Salad:

¾ to 1 cup stemmed arugula
4 ounces fresh goat cheese, crumbled
Freshly ground black pepper
2 teaspoons extra-virgin olive oil

1. To cook the potatoes, preheat the oven to 300°F.

2. In a roasting pan, toss the potatoes with the garlic cloves, salt to taste, and olive oil. Bake for 1½ to 2 hours until the potatoes are fork tender. Check the potatoes every so often and if they stick to the bottom of the pan, scrape them from the pan and gently toss them with the other ingredients. Lower the heat to 250°F if the potatoes are cooking too quickly.

3. To make the vinaigrette, whisk the mustard and vinegar together in a small bowl. Slowly add the olive oil, whisking constantly, until the vinaigrette thickens.

4. To make the salad, take the potatoes from the oven and scrape them into a large bowl. Pour the vinaigrette over the warm potatoes and gently toss them with the dressing. Add the arugula and toss again.

5. Heap the potato salad into a shallow bowl or onto a large platter. Sprinkle the crumbled cheese over the top. Season with pepper and drizzle with olive oil. Serve the salad warm or at room temperature.

Mussels Provençale

Serves 6

This classic dish is always excellent. It's so easy to prepare and you can make it nearly anytime you see fresh, shiny black mussels piled in the fish store. In the springtime I use imported plum tomatoes, but in the height of the summer, I rely instead on five or six fragrant vine-ripened tomatoes. Serve the heady stew in oversized soup bowls along with crusty bread for dipping.

3 pounds fresh mussels in shells
¼ cup olive oil
½ cup thinly sliced onions (about 1 small onion)
4 cloves garlic, thinly sliced
1 cup dry white wine
1 can (28 ounces) plum tomatoes, undrained, or 3½ cups
chopped fresh tomatoes (about 7 large tomatoes)
½ cup chopped fresh parsley
2 tablespoons thinly sliced fresh basil leaves or 1 teaspoon dried basil

1.   Scrub the mussels thoroughly under cold running water and rinse them in several changes of water. Using a wire brush or pad, remove the beards from the mussels.

2.   Heat the oil in a large saucepan or stockpot over medium heat. Add the onion and garlic and sauté for about 5 minutes until the onion is softened and slightly golden; take care not to burn the garlic. Add the wine and tomatoes. Cover and cook over high heat for 2 to 3 minutes until boiling.

3.   Add the mussels, parsley, and basil to the boiling tomato mixture. Cover, reduce the heat slightly to medium-high, and let the mussels steam for about 5 minutes until they open. Discard any that do not open.

4.   Spoon the mussels and tomato broth into soup bowls and serve piping hot.

Grilled Tuna with Tomato-Cilantro Salsa

Serves 6

With the freshest summer vegetables, a sharp knife, and a little imagination, you can create a warm-weather salsa to go with grilled fish, as I have here, or to serve with chips or sliced, raw vegetables. I especially like to make an afternoon of it, inviting my houseguests or other friends into the kitchen for a relaxed chop-and-gossip session. Be sure to give the salsa time to mellow before serving, but for fresh flavor and crisp texture, serve on the same day it's made. For this salsa, I use red and yellow peppers combined with deep-red tomatoes, bright-green cilantro, and soft-green scallions. You may vary the color and amount of ingredients to suit your own taste.

1 tablespoon dry mustard
¼ cup white wine vinegar
6 tablespoons extra-virgin olive oil
3 medium tomatoes (about 2 pounds), coarsely chopped
1 red bell pepper, seeded, deveined and finely chopped,
1 yellow bell pepper, seeded, deveined, and finely chopped
4 scallions (white and green parts), finely chopped
½ cup finely chopped cilantro
Salt and freshly ground pepper
6 1-inch-thick tuna steaks (about 2¼ pounds)

1. To make the salsa, whisk the mustard and vinegar together in a small bowl. Slowly add the olive oil, whisking constantly, until the vinaigrette thickens. Stir in the tomatoes, peppers, scallions, and cilantro. Mix well. Season to taste with salt and pepper. Let the salsa sit at room temperature for at least 2 hours to give the flavors time to blend.

2.   Prepare a charcoal or gas grill. When the coals are medium hot, grill the tuna for 6 to 7 minutes on each side until flaky but still moist.

3.   Spoon some salsa into the center of each plate. Place a tuna steak on top of it and spoon more salsa over the fish. Serve immediately.

Grilled Swordfish Kebabs

Serves 6

*Fish and vegetable kebabs are absolutely wonderful and lots of fun to grill.
Do not let the swordfish marinate for longer than three hours or its texture will
soften. Serve these with yellow rice or tabbouleh and salad.*

Juice of 1 lemon
Salt and freshly ground black pepper
½ teaspoon dried oregano
¼ cup coarsely chopped fresh parsley
½ cup olive oil
2 pounds 1½-inch-thick swordfish steaks
2 medium-size red onions, quartered
2 red bell peppers, seeded, deveined, and cut into 1½-inch squares
12 wooden skewers, soaked in water for 1 hour

1.   To make the marinade, combine the lemon juice, salt and pepper to
taste, oregano, and parsley in a food processor or blender and process
until the parsley is finely chopped. With the machine running, slowly add
the olive oil. When all the oil is incorporated, set the marinade aside.

2.   Trim the swordfish of any skin and fat. Cut it into 1½-inch cubes. Lay
them in a shallow glass or ceramic dish and pour the marinade over them.
Cover and refrigerate for 2 to 3 hours.

3.   Separate the onion quarters into single pieces and toss them with the
peppers in a bowl. Add a little olive oil to the vegetables.

4.   Prepare a charcoal or gas grill.

5.   Make 6 kebabs, using 2 skewers for each one. The 2 skewers should be parallel with approximately ½-inch between them. Double skewers make handling the kebabs on the grill easy. Thread the skewers with alternating pieces of fish and vegetables, beginning and ending with fish. There should be enough for about 5 pieces of swordfish on each double skewer.

6.   Grill the kebabs 5 or 6 inches from medium-hot coals for about 10 minutes, turning them once or twice, until cooked through and no longer pink on the inside. Slide the fish and vegetables off the skewers directly onto each plate.

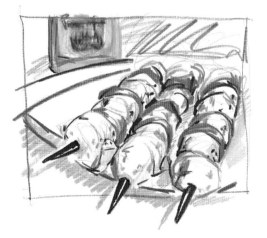

Classic Barbecued Chicken

Serves 6 to 8

Barbecued chicken is a summertime tradition all across America. I've tried lots of different recipes and after some experimentation, came up with this variation on an old southern recipe. The secret is to marinate the chicken overnight in a light brew of vinegar, water, and spicy whole cloves and then baste it with the barbecue sauce during the last half of cooking. Grill the chicken over slow-burning coals; be sure they are covered with white ash before putting the chicken on the grill. Otherwise, it will cook too fast.

2½ cups white wine vinegar
4 cups water
12 whole cloves
Salt and freshly ground black pepper
2 frying chickens (2½ to 3 pounds each), cut into pieces
2 tablespoons corn oil
2 cloves garlic, thinly sliced
⅓ cup thinly sliced yellow onion (about 1 small onion)
1½ cups tomato ketchup
½ cup packed brown sugar
1 teaspoon Dijon mustard
2 tablespoons Worcestershire sauce
Juice of ½ lemon
1 teaspoon Tabasco sauce
2 teaspoons chili powder

1.   The day before serving, combine the vinegar with the water, cloves, and salt and pepper to taste in a shallow glass or ceramic bowl. Add the chicken pieces and turn several times to coat. Cover and refrigerate. Let the chicken marinate for 8 hours or overnight, turning it occasionally

2. To make the barbecue sauce, heat the oil in a large skillet. Sauté the sliced garlic and onion for about 5 minutes over medium-high heat until golden; take care the garlic does not burn. Add the ketchup, sugar, mustard, Worcestershire sauce, lemon juice, Tabasco sauce, and chili powder. Stir constantly until the sauce comes to a simmer. Reduce the heat to low and cook for 45 minutes to 1 hour, stirring occasionally. Remove from heat and let cool.

3. Prepare a charcoal or gas grill.

4. When the coals are covered with white ash, lift the chicken from the marinade and grill over the low heat for about 15 minutes, turning frequently for even cooking. Cook for another 15 to 25 minutes, basting with the sauce, until the chicken is done.

5. Serve the chicken with the remaining barbecue sauce.

Grilled Steak with Port Marinade

Serves 6

*Summer just wouldn't be summer without grilled steak. Marinating the beef in
full-bodied port mixed with a little fresh rosemary tenderizes the meat while
adding appealing piquancy. For the best flavor, marinate the steak for at least
two hours. If you use top round or flank steak—tougher cuts than sirloin—you
might want to marinate the meat for a few hours longer.*

2 tablespoons olive oil
Juice of ½ lemon
1 teaspoon sugar
1 tablespoon chopped fresh rosemary or 1 teaspoon dried rosemary
4 cloves garlic, thinly slice
1 cup port
Freshly ground black pepper
3 pounds 1-inch-thick sirloin, top round, or flank steak

1.   To make the marinade, combine in a small bowl, the olive oil, lemon
juice, sugar, rosemary, garlic, port, and pepper to taste.

2. Put the steak in a glass or ceramic dish and pour the marinade over it.
Cover and refrigerate for at least 2 hours and up to 8 hours. Turn the
steak occasionally.

3.   Prepare a charcoal or gas grill. Grill the steak over medium-hot
coals for 4 to 5 minutes to a side for rare and 6 to 7 minutes for medium.
Baste several times during grilling with the marinade.

4. Remove the steak to a platter and slice on the diagonal into ⅜-inch
slices. Pour any accumulated juices on the platter over the meat and serve.

Penne with Fresh Tomato and Basil Sauce

Serves 6

Because tomatoes are at their very best in mid to late summer, I like to use them whenever possible. Nothing compares with a vine-ripened August tomato plucked from the garden or purchased at the local farmers market. This redolent, quick sauce, which marries tomatoes with their natural partner, basil, can be made while the pasta water heats.

⅓ cup plus 1 tablespoon olive oil
6 cloves garlic, thinly sliced
4 pounds tomatoes (10 to 12 medium tomatoes), quartered
6 tablespoons coarsely chopped fresh basil
Salt and freshly ground black pepper
1 teaspoon sugar
1 pound penne
Fresh basil leaves, for garnish
Freshly grated Parmesan cheese

1. Heat ⅓ cup of the olive oil in a large skillet over medium heat. Add the garlic and sauté for 2 to 3 minutes until golden; take care the garlic does not burn.

2. Add the tomatoes, chopped basil, salt and pepper to taste, and sugar. Simmer gently over medium-low heat for about 15 minutes until slightly thickened. Stir occasionally.

3. While the sauce simmers, bring a large pot of lightly salted water to a boil. Add the remaining tablespoon of olive oil. Add the penne and cook for 10 to 12 minutes until al dente. Drain the pasta.

4. Spoon the penne onto warmed plates. Top each serving with sauce and garnish with basil leaves. Serve with freshly grated Parmesan cheese.

Summer Corn with Sugar Snap Peas

Serves 6

*My family and I never tire of Long Island's legendary sweet corn during July
and August. Trips to the farm stand become an almost daily ritual and while
we usually eat the tender ears boiled with a little butter and salt, I came up
with this fast, easy dish one day when I couldn't resist the sugar snap
peas. It quickly became a summertime favorite.*

I pound sugar snap peas, ends snapped off
2 tablespoons unsalted butter
I tablespoon olive oil
3 cups fresh corn kernels (from 3 ears sweet corn)
Salt and freshly ground black pepper
¼ cup chopped fresh parsley

1.   Bring a saucepan of lightly salted water to a boil. Add the peas, lower the heat, and simmer for no longer than 2 minutes. Drain immediately.

2.   Heat the butter and oil in a skillet over medium-high heat. Add the drained peas, corn, and salt and pepper to taste. Stir constantly for 1 minute. Add the parsley and cook, stirring, for another minute. Serve immediately.

Blueberry Peach Cake

Serves 6 to 8

When peaches and blueberries are at their peak, no other fruit compares with them. Combine them and you taste summertime. This no-fuss cake is a good way to make the most of their abundance during their all-too-brief season. The peaches complement the berrries and both taste wonderful nestled on a sweet, plain cake. This is a great choice to take along for a picnic, but it is also just right eaten on the back porch after the sun goes down. Try it with a scoop of vanilla ice cream—or maybe homemade peach ice cream.

Butter and flour, for baking dish
1 cup sifted all-purpose flour
1 teaspoon baking powder
½ cup (1 stick) unsalted butter, softened
½ cup firmly packed light brown sugar
½ cup plus 3 tablespoons granulated sugar
2 large eggs
2 cups peeled and thinly sliced ripe peaches (2 to 3 peaches)
1 cup fresh blueberries
1 tablespoon fresh lemon juice
½ teaspoon ground cinnamon

1. Preheat the oven to 350°F. Lightly butter and flour an 8-inch square baking pan.

2. In a medium bowl, whisk together the flour and baking powder.

3. In a large bowl, using an electric mixer set at high, cream the butter, brown sugar, and ½ cup of the granulated sugar for about 3 minutes until light and fluffy.

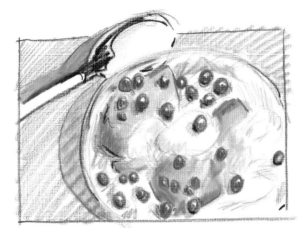

4.   With the mixer running and set at medium, add the flour mixture to the batter, a little at a time; do not overmix. Beat in the eggs.

5.   Scrape the batter into the prepared pan. Smooth the surface and then arrange the sliced peaches and blueberries on top of the batter. Sprinkle with lemon juice. In a small bowl, combine the remaining 3 tablespoons sugar with the cinnamon and sprinkle the mixture over the fruit. Bake for about 1 hour until the cake begins to pull away from the sides of the pan and turns golden brown.

6.   Let the cake cool in the pan set on a wire rack. When completely cool, serve the cake directly from the pan or lift it out, cut it into squares and serve it fruit-side up.

Frosted Cherries and Mint

Serves 6

This is one of my favorite ways to serve sweet, fresh cherries. The mint leaves, mingling with the cherries and crushed ice, flavor the fruit just enough so that you get a cool hint of mint. I like to pack this mixture in a large plastic container with a tight-fitting lid and take it to the beach in the cooler. The cold cherries are more refreshing than ice pops. I have included instructions for crushing ice in the food processor or blender. Both do a very good job; so does hurling a bag of ice against the deck!

12 ice cubes
1 pound ripe cherries
½ cup thinly sliced fresh mint leaves

1.   Crush the ice in the blender by filling the cannister about
¾ full of ice cubes. Turn the blender on high and grind up the ice.
Depending on the size of the cannister, you may have to do this in
2 batches. You can crush the ice in a food processor, too, but take care it
does not turn to ice water.

2.   Fill a large bowl with the crushed ice, cherries, and mint. Toss together.
Refrigerate for at least 1 hour and serve chilled.

Summer Birthday Cake
with Whipped Cream and Peaches

Serves 12 to 16

My younger daughter, Isabelle, had the good sense to be born in the summer. We celebrate her birthday every year on the lawn of our house in Montauk, crowning the lovely afternoon with this light white cake frosted with nothing more exotic than freshly whipped cream and served with summer's best juicy, sweet peaches. Although you can frost the cake and refrigerate it before serving, it will not hold up for more than two or three hours.

Butter and flour, for preparing cake pans
3 cups sifted all-purpose flour
1 tablespoon baking powder
½ teaspoon salt
¾ cup (1½ sticks) unsalted butter, softened
2 cups sugar
1 teaspoon vanilla extract
1 cup milk
6 large egg whites, at room temperature
1 cup heavy cream
8 or 9 ripe peaches, peeled and sliced into thin wedges

1. Preheat the oven to 375°F. Butter and lightly flour two 9-inch cake pans. Shake out any excess flour.

2. In a large bowl, whisk together the flour, baking powder, and salt.

3.   In another large bowl, using an electric mixer set at high, cream the butter and 1½ cups of the sugar for about 2 minutes until light and fluffy. Add the vanilla and beat until just combined.

4.   With the mixer running and set at medium, add about ¾ cup of the flour mixture and then mix in ¼ cup of the milk. Repeat 3 times until all the flour is used. Beat just until the batter is smooth. Do not overmix.

5.   Using a large, clean dry bowl and clean dry beaters, beat the egg whites until foamy with an electric mixer set at medium-high speed. Increase the speed to high and slowly add the remaining ½ cup sugar. Beat the meringue to stiff peaks.

continued

6.   Fold the meringue into the cake batter. Do not overfold; you will be able to see whites in the batter.

7.   Pour the batter into the prepared pans. Smooth the top of the batter with a spatula. Bake the cake layers for 30 to 35 minutes until a cake tester or toothpick inserted in the centers comes out clean and the cakes are lightly brown and begin to pull away from the sides of the pans.

8.   Let the cake layers cool in their pans for 4 or 5 minutes. Loosen the edges with a kitchen knife and invert the layers onto wire racks to cool completely.

9.   Shortly before serving, whip the cream with an electric mixer set at high speed. Rotate the mixer with a circular motion until the cream is lightly whipped. It does not have to be stiff but should hold its shape when mounded.

10.   Spread the cream between the cooled cake layers and over the sides and top of the cake. Serve at once or refrigerate up to several hours until serving. Before serving, decorate the top of the cake with some peach slices, if desired. Serve each piece with sliced peaches.

RECIPE INDEX

TABLE OF EQUIVALENTS

The exact equivalents in the following tables have been rounded for convenience.

OVEN TEMPERATURES			WEIGHTS		LENGTH MEASURES		LIQUIDS		
Fahrenheit	Celsius	Gas	US/UK	Metric			US	Metric	UK
250	120	½	1oz	30g	⅛in	3mm	2tbl	30ml	1fl oz
275	140	1	2oz	60g	¼in	6mm	¼ cup	60ml	2fl oz
300	150	2	3oz	90g	½ in	12mm	⅓ cup	80ml	3fl oz
325	160	3	4oz (¼ lb)	125g	1in	2.5cm	½ cup	125ml	4fl oz
350	180	4	5oz (⅓lb)	155g	2in	5cm	⅔ cup	160ml	5fl oz
375	190	5	6oz	185g	3in	7.5cm	¾ cup	180ml	6fl oz
400	200	6	7oz	220g	4in	10cm	1 cup	250ml	8fl oz
425	220	7	8oz (½lb)	250g	5in	13cm	1½ cup	375ml	12fl oz
450	230	8	10oz	315g	6in	15cm	2 cups	500ml	16fl oz
475	240	9	12oz (¾lb)	375g	7in	18cm	4 cups/1qt	1l	32fl oz
500	260	10	14oz	440g	8in	20cm			
			16oz (1lb)	500g	9in	23cm			
			1½lb	750g	10in	25cm			
			2lb	1kg	11in	28cm			
			3lb	1.5kg	12in	30cm